through injured eyes

(...clear intuition assumed)

poetry by
michael sean gardner

Order this book online at www.trafford.com/08-0803
or email orders@trafford.com

Most Trafford titles are also available at major online book retailers.

© Copyright 2008 Micheal Sean Gardner.

All rights reserved. No part of this publication may be reproduced, stored in a retrieval system, or transmitted, in any form or by any means, electronic, mechanical, photocopying, recording, or otherwise, without the written prior permission of the author.

Edited by: Joyce Nunn & Christopher Tiessen
Cover Design/ Artwork by: Christopher Tiessen
Designed by: Christopher Tiessen
Photography by: Christopher Tiessen

Note for Librarians: A cataloguing record for this book is available from Library and Archives Canada at www.collectionscanada.ca/amicus/index-e.html

Printed in Victoria, BC, Canada.

ISBN: 978-1-4251-8134-5

We at Trafford believe that it is the responsibility of us all, as both individuals and corporations, to make choices that are environmentally and socially sound. You, in turn, are supporting this responsible conduct each time you purchase a Trafford book, or make use of our publishing services. To find out how you are helping, please visit www.trafford.com/responsiblepublishing.html

Our mission is to efficiently provide the world's finest, most comprehensive book publishing service, enabling every author to experience success. To find out how to publish your book, your way, and have it available worldwide, visit us online at www.trafford.com/10510

 www.trafford.com

North America & international
toll-free: 1 888 232 4444 (USA & Canada)
phone: 250 383 6864 ♦ fax: 250 383 6804 ♦ email: info@trafford.com

The United Kingdom & Europe
phone: +44 (0)1865 487 395 ♦ local rate: 0845 230 9601
facsimile: +44 (0)1865 481 507 ♦ email: info.uk@trafford.com

10 9 8 7 6 5 4 3

Through Injured Eyes is a collection of poetic prose that has served as an outlet for me to flush so many thoughts that attempted to put out the fire of my authentic life. I would like to dedicate this effort to my inspirations Francesca and Nicole; to some of my family and some of my friends; to love felt for special women; and to a person who gave me strength, love, and the opportunity to open my injured eyes – my mother.

"Treat people as if they were what they ought to be; then help them become what they are capable of being." Ashleigh Briliant

table of contents

volume one: "the early years"   13

worst enemy   15
will you think it?   16
to exercise the mind   17
there is something;   19
the locker room   20
the blessing   21
the balcony   22
symposium   23
so hard   25
run away   26
realizations   28
moments   29
mind power   30
hopeless romantic   31
knights gambit   32
is media the message?   33
great provider   35
feeling alive   36
fear of pain   37
every castle   39
cyclic change   40
the realization   42

volume two: "inspirations"   45

embodying beauty   47
you inspire   48
why do hearts ache?   49
belief   50
reasons   51
feelings once upon a time   52
miracle worker   53

keylynn lorain	54
exhilaration	56
can you	57
chivalry dead	58
true exhilarations	59
overanxious	60
poetic mastery	61
noticing	62
pondering retribution	63
silhouettes generate cognition	64
the absence	65
the oracle transpires reality	66
unobstructed vision	67
mind power	68
security gives birth to stability	69
a b c's for u	70
is truth dead?	71
distance	72
that one	73
train motion	74
defining cool	75
e-ma-ho	76
nodi	77
sympathetic yet pragmatic	78
experiences	79
true contentment	80
the choice	81
in the morning	82
studying life & love	83
needs in life	84
capturing insight	85
family	86
the apology	87
use the sword	88
grins overwhelming	89
possibilities	90
inspirations	91
that face	92

volume three: "haiku"   95

careful investigation	97
choices	97
untitled	97
fatigue	97
untitled	98
finding reality	98
got to believe	98
idea's road map	98
indecision	99
jedi ways	99
lent	99
love	99
love's truth	100
lust	100
nature	100
nava armani	100
naveed	101
nudity	101
plan for survival	101
poetic ability	101
soul mate	102
untitled	102
the white stump	102
writing	102
personal gift	103
cranial strength	103

forward

January 11, 1999 was the day that altered my perceptions forever. After a fine Portuguese dinner at my one-time girlfriend's parents' home a ride back to my university residence was in order. Like so many times before we reversed out of the inclined driveway and my girlfriend shifted into gear. The distance that we had to travel was by no means a lengthy journey often thought to be associated with tragedy. Instead, there were maybe only fifteen minutes of road between her parents' home and the apartment I was living in during my second year of university studies in the Faculty of Engineering. However, the usual fifteen minutes soon needed to be recalculated as we took in to account the snowstorm punishing the urban landscape that evening.

The snow-covered journey was never completed that night and never would be. Less than half of the way home my girlfriend lost control of her vehicle and slid off the road. Her pathetically-small car hit a snow bank and – like the steel ball bearing of a pinball arcade game – rebounded immediately and spun across the road. The out-of-control car finally did come to a halt as it collided with an oncoming van. The resulting accident was horrific and – like the car that crushed to a sudden halt upon impact – my life as I knew it also came to an abrupt halt.

Destroyed in the dissipation of energy that occurred was: a shattered pelvis; a tib-fib fracture in my right leg; a broken right clavicle; a slit urethra from a razor-sharp bone fragment that had once been my pelvis; and last but surely not least the traumatic brain injury. The swelling of my injured brain imprisoned me in a coma for nearly three months. My lifeless body in such need of medical attention had to be transported by ambulance first to the Kitchener-Waterloo hospital to be stabilized and then – once stabilized – on to the specialized neurological traumatic medical attention at Hamilton General hospital. The emergent blizzard that night was so ferocious that the trip from the K-W hospital to the Hamilton General could not be made by air in a helicopter. Instead, an ambulance had to carefully navigate the fifty-minute journey from K-W to Hamilton in those treacherous conditions with my parents following in their Jeep as close as possible.

In April 1999 my eyes struggled to open after the long rest in a comatose state and my choice to attempt recovery was made. Nine years have elapsed and a new life has materialized from the ashes of my former existence. Many obstacles have been met living this new existence and many hurdles overcome with the strength of attitude, determination to succeed, and the support that was felt along with the energy that was used to heal. Support is a choice – the choice to accept it allows the support to be realized. Feeling and realizing the presence of a divine energy at those most painful moments during this recovery has been comforting and necessary for me. The major supports in rebuilding a life from the single heart beat that kept me alive were strong relationships with my rehabilitation team; invaluable relationships with some friends; and love and energy provided by most of my family. In particular, it was my mother who witnessed her son die and then watched just as intently as he chose to come back to life.

I firmly believe that these poems can free your mind and bring awareness of the energy that exists all around you. When the energy is understood to exist in every single thing the ability to truly understand is achieved. The poetic literature that follows is a direct result of how life is seen through injured eyes.

Michael Sean Gardner, 2008.

volume one:
"the early years"

worst enemy

Your own mind is one of your worst enemies,
It is something very capable of making you weak in the knees,
Whether it be regarding your education or the relationship that just ended
your mind can be that one acknowledgement of comfort that you so
desperately seek,
A scholar once noted, "If you can't change your circumstance; change your
perspective",
Basing his clever thought simply on the power of the mind,
A divine mystery is hidden inside the mass of nerves firing repetitively,
Today's society is focused on whatever it takes to render the mind euphoric,
Alcohol, drugs, sex, and even money tempts the mind much like the serpent
tempted Adam to bite the apple,
A placebo pill that can counter these desires is very simple and is just
keeping occupied,
An occupied mind cannot stray from the righteous path,
Learning to enjoy whatever is keeping you occupied is a secret of happiness,
A secret of sanity,
Try Smiling once in a while simply for the wonder you feel in return,
And if this routine becomes habit then your worst enemy, ego, will burn.

07/06/04

will you think it?

Looking for that thought that has never been thunk,
Almost as hard as meeting someone who doesn't know that the color of his own blood is red,
To plagiarize is to steal something someone else has already thunk,
It seems sometimes almost impossible to come up with new thought,
Similar to meeting someone that didn't know the fate of the Titanic,
Well my friend, it's common knowledge,
Everybody knows she Sunk!

Thinking that epochal thought that could save the planet,
Is something that seems very hard,
Almost like searching for a glass of water in a desert,
Like learning to speak again or walk again after injury,
Or even as hard as escaping from prison right under the nose of the guard.

But it can be done, I promise you this,
We just have to sit quietly and allow our thoughts to turn into our own minds,
And when the answer becomes clear the feeling of accomplishment will suffocate,
And all you will experience is total Bliss!

12/06/03

to exercise the mind

Do you sleep well?
Do you know how to relax?
Can you turn your mind off?
The mind - a powerful tool we've got - understanding its full potential is
important.

We all go through life existing with what we've got, on a schedule that is
repetitious; perhaps provoking you to want to yell,
Cursing about your job, or your friends, or the mere fact that you need to pay
the tax,
To shut down your mind is an incredible gift because avoiding this act will
lead straight to mental exhaustion.
As a body builder strengthening his muscles, the brain needs to be stressed
to eventually grow.
Without this prompting *le cerveau* lies forever dormant,

The mind is a tool that is often abused,
With either drugs or alcohol, belief or habit,
The mind is an innocent bystander when the actions you choose to entertain
lead to becoming an addict,
So many options are present to us it is disheartening the right path is rarely
pursued.

To fully fatigue your mind force it to flex; partake in activities in which you
struggle,
Completing a task to its end will allow a feeling of accomplishment and
inspire the feeling of something special,
Choosing what releases endorphins will not always be beneficial,
The more challenging road will evoke feelings of satisfaction while the easy
road will eventually lead to trouble,

Exhausting the mind will inspire deep rest,
A place where every aspect in your life is brought down a notch,
Amazingly this simple step is often overlooked and we choose to bring
everything to the red line,
Just being calm and composed will allow you to function at your best,

05/12/05

there is something;

I can't explain it but that emotion fills me like Italian food consumed during
November,
When it's cold outside and you want to be that one who offers warmth,
The warmth that can be found only in your arms waiting to embrace,
You're difficult when you're honest; like a piece of glass left out on the beach,
It's like an accident waiting to happen; almost ironic,
Going so long you run out of room; even if you catch the ball it will be called
back because you're in unchartered territory,
Why do our minds tease us in this way?

One followed by another the words don't seem to come,
Fulfilling the wants is such a daunting task when what you really want is
something not so lean,
It is like that question on the exam that just can not be answered,
You know you want to be more than nothing so what can you be?
Who do you feel like you have to impress,
The answer you're looking for evades you like a child caught up in a game of
Hide & Seek.

Something is yet to be discovered but you don't hold any credentials to
render yourself serious,
Do you need a degree to confirm your God given task,
The answer to the riddle is blowing in the wind; you just have to hear it,
What entices you to listen and what makes you want to speak?
Not knowing the future is challenging but you can't complain,
Knowing stuff would take the fun out of the game and maybe let you realize
your gift,
The Lord works in mysterious ways that aren't easily discerned,
Life is about choices and whatever is the outcome you will take with you
what you've learned.

11/18/05

the locker room

That place where all inequalities are dropped is the place where equality thrives.
A place where belonging is as common as mosquitoes are in the north.
All fronts are left on the outside where trouble persists but entering the haven
is moving into a reality where dogs and cats can coexist,
The institution like atmosphere conjures the feelings of belonging
reminiscent of blood,
Where language connotes the idea that all have gathered to improve their lives,

A locker in a general area acts as home-base for the time to follow where
exhaustion, sweat, and motivation are exercised.
In the tin box, day to day attitude is shed and a new more confident self
emerges.
Locked up for a time, the attitude fits differently after the grueling regime
that will be undertaken,
All in the hopes that your body's goals will be realized,

Weight training is one aspect of the feat, like the climax of a saga,
Like the solid rocks that build a wall the edifice needs mortar to make it hold,
The cement that binds the muscles in form can be summarized with cardio-
vascular exercise,
What society views as attractive is the reason for some explanation in the
quest for health,
At this point the body is exuding lactic acid; awaiting the return to the locker
room; signifying the demise,

The sense of accomplishment boils over during return to the safe haven,
The emperor's new clothes are now something real; leaving little to dispute,
The body thirsts for rejuvenation and waits to be satisfied,
In the gallery where protein powders look to be ingested and metamorphose
to become part of your own,
That mass produced plastic chair, at that moment in time, is very reminiscent
of a majestic throne,

05/16/05

the blessing

What's in a savior?
What's in the one thing that so many take for granted,
What's in somebody that inspires and shines at every moment,
What's the one thing that can make you feel like a million bucks but doesn't
cost a thing,
The same answer rings true in every question and it's simple to acquire,
Love is the answer; and it's what propels me through the labyrinth I find
myself in,
It's what allows me to break muscle then make muscle,
It gives me the endurance to pursue everything that because of you is now
within reach,
You are a blessing to me that never seems to expire,
With lots of love you teach me to fight Fire with Fire.

27/05/06

the balcony

The location where the heart and mind are in unison and parole is
experienced rather than spoken,
A place where hearts are made whole by the one God has placed on the earth
to complete my soul,
When completion of the soul occurs the sensations are euphoric,
Like a noble knight saving a damsel in distress the endorphins evoked by
that moment are truly heroic,
Where two beings are connected through words as magnets connect through
that mysterious attraction,
Oh great distance that exists between the lips,
Like static holds lint to a sweater I dream of allowing the distance to
evaporate like a puddle under the sun,
To be allowed to let the puddle run dry signifies a meeting of the lips and the
disclosing of all,
With the exchange of energy passed from mouth to mouth there is an
unspoken agreement made,
Like an oath taken in court or when the first brick of an edifice is laid,
The commitment to completion and creation of the new castle is understood
and the journey down the Yellow Brick road begins,
To ecstasy this road leads and both travelers do know,
Along the way there are distractions much like the bright red candy apple to
an innocent child,
A strong mind can overcome these temptations and act like a compass
guiding towards your destiny,
With one simple word I might be heart broken,
But with one simple word the game will be won,
The question to provoke these answers is quite simple and fills me with glee,
Penelope, I am asking you if you will marry me?

22/04/05

symposium

The establishment nestled in the heart of uptown Waterloo evoked countless
emotion,
Feeling completely at ease dictated my conduct that must have been noticed,
The energy present at the little table was quite astonishing.
It is miraculous how simplicity can conjure up dream-like sensations,
A night that started by good fortune continued with the potency of an elixir
or a potion,

Waiting in the back where the energy was allowed for the walk very similar
to the one taken down the aisle,
The mood at the table very reminiscent of the anticipation of opening a
special gift,
The feelings were reflected with the precision of a laser light trapped in a
cube of mirrors,
For the entire evening satisfying conversation took place only interrupted by
the presence of a smile,

Feelings of pleasantries were experienced from the onset of the evening to
order placement,
The sentiment was further enhanced in item selection being everything from
complete satisfaction to something more historic,
Simplicity was the notion that attracted attention and created the need to
further our understanding,
The exchange of heart felt stories let time pass quickly bringing our selves
more adjacent,

Conclusion of dinner led to the acknowledgement of what was next,
The first suggestion was a dessert to share, leaving my mind angling for
reason,
Ordering a second espresso was my course of action, trying to dull my mind,
Perplexed I made a necessary suggestion of my own-a dessert; each was the
only answer that would put to rest the hunger effects,

Taste buds being active, memories were simultaneously called to mind,
Indulging in New York style cheese cake drummed thoughts of living like
Gotti or Capone,

The character identity filled me with an understanding of the way things
could be and I inhaled deeply to get the best of the moment,
At that moment realizing the truth of a love for life all gained while we dined,

27/04/05

so hard

It's so hard and it's getting even harder,
To live out this existence where everything is secretly working against you,
When nothing works; not relationships or friendships or even your own body,
At the end of the day you sometimes want to call it quits,
But unfortunately that's not acceptable,
For many reasons you must go on, fight another day, die another day,
The question is posed, "Whom do you believe in? Is it money or God?"
Either way you're "Up the creek without a paddle",
You choose money to be on your side then your faith suffers,
And if you're truly walking with God your financial security diminishes,
Why can't you have the best of both worlds?
Because in the end it all works in balance,
A little bit of this, a little bit of that; it is crucial that you are familiar with both emotions,
If you try to cheat the scales and get more than your share of a feeling,
Then the emotion you seek to live in will become normalized and it will lose its appeal,
As Sigmund Freud explained about happiness, there are three forces working against us,
The supreme power of nature,
The inadequacies of our own bodies,
And the feebleness we notice in our social relationships, or friendships,
Remedying any one force will permit life in a utopian society,
This is because of how our minds work,
All we need is one positive event to capture our attention and the entire day will follow suit,
The positive event can be as simple as a cookie,
Anything that acts as nourishment will act as the means to an end and lift you high,
Not in a narcotic sense but something purely innocent,
All leaders should sit down together and eat to return to innocence.

14/04/04

run away

The feeling of suffocation creeps near whenever the labels emerge,
The muscles contract and the airway constricts,
What is the solution to the dilemma? is it attainable? is it within reach?
The only thing that's real and makes sense is enlightenment; catastrophic
injury is something I wish to purge.

No matter how hard I try this classification can't be beat,
Why this is true is pretty easy to understand,
The simple fact being the power of the mind to create your world is not such
an astonishing feat,
What you choose to surround yourself with is of vital importance; as is Shaq
to the Miami Heat,
No matter how you play the game, all roads lead to Perdition and this one
leads to defeat,

It is all in what you listen to and the game is yours to play,
Listen to the whispers and you can believe that tomorrow will be a better day,
rejecting all dismay,
Surround yourself with motivational powers that will urge you to seize the day,
By keeping your mind occupied with thoughts other than worry it's a sure
thing you'll find your way,

Just be sure your magazine is opened to the right page because you wouldn't
want to read the wrong story and refuse the invitations your mind submits,
Your personality evokes feelings but are they what you need,
To be categorized as something that lacks is difficult to endure,
It has been bestowed upon you-the ability to create a cure,

To run away is the easy way out,
You were put in this situation because you can bring about positive change,
Sometimes it's hard to change the situation where you might feel like a captive,
If you can't change the circumstance it's easy to change your perspective,

The feeling of suffocation creeps near whenever the labels emerge,
The muscles contract and the airway constricts,
What is the solution to the dilemma? is it attainable? is it within reach?
The only thing that's real and makes sense is enlightenment; catastrophic
injury is something I wish to purge.

27/05/05

realizations

Understanding that you're in this game for a set amount of time sometimes causes insecurities,
Most people ignore these feelings labeling them as "Distant Future Events",
Coming close to the end once forces one to realize,
The realization that your previous life may have been going down the wrong path,
Previous in the sense that you got a second chance and better get down on your knees and give thanks.

The realization that comes with another shot at the game is very real and life altering,
The shedding of your former self occurs much like used skin that comes off a snake,
Growing the new skin is difficult and takes much patience,
One must alter their own thinking and really believe they can accomplish anything.

Sometimes to actually make your realizations a reality some help is necessary to accept,
The help usually comes from members of your very own family if they are capable and willing,
Being careful of such retributions requires the unspoken secret to be kept.

5/8/05

moments

Searching meticulously for that one moment to start being who you always dream you can be,
Moments come and moments go; it's all in the selection of the moment that matters,
With the realization that every moment counts your self is filled with uncertainty,
That moment when you discover you already have the key to the barred entrance will be significant,
Like Einstein's "Eureka" total satisfaction will encompass your being and you will see the road ahead with great precision,
Like the sense of accomplishment that comes with the reception of a fantastic performance worked for diligently,
Or the moment when the taste of something is registered in the brain as Good,
When you realize you yourself are the Master Puppeteer, the power you hold will be immeasurable,
You did hear me right. The Master Puppeteer is you and you are your own Bestselling author,
Believe that the moment has come and use its strength to compose your next moment,
When you string those moments together like the one who strings pearls you have no choice but to live the authentic existence,
Valuing everything that is good allows you to be great,
Make that step and move into your omnipotent position,
The moment to harness the knowledge of your power is something to endow,
Your time to shine my friend is and has always been right now,

22/04/05

mind power

What has become apparent to me is the power of your very own mind,
This mass of nerves, like jelly, runs the show and is the control center;
kind of like Star Trek's helm,
Many believe it is the heart that gives you vitality and it does when the
microscope is on zoom,
Many of us live our lives on zoom as though we are afraid to step back and
see the whole picture,
Like the work of art done in Pointillism, when in focus all that can be seen is
a bunch of dots,
It is necessary to take a step back to get full appreciation where innocent
dots morph into a work of art,
Backing up from the depended on set of rules allows you to gain an
understanding of the possibilities,
This then leads to new thought that may end up saving us from ourselves,
The mind is delicate like a fragile egg and when broken it is believed it
cannot be repaired,
The options of course are two fold leaving the decision to you,
Either give up and let yourself down or exercise patience and commit to
rebuilding your life,
La Reine Rouge avez me montre comment utiliser l'energie le 26 avrile
2004 avec l'amour,
It is I who owe her the luxuries I understand that society as a whole takes for
granted,
At that moment in time the world was a happy place and to stay in the
queen's presence longer is all I wanted,
She was shining and I wanted to shine too; that's all I'm saying dog,
I feel that I want to be the one that guides her through the fog,
We'll see how the story plays out only with how I felt that day in my mind
there is no doubt,
Because I believe the mind holds the power my actions might go against the
rules and I know I'm being smart,
It is true that sometimes you just have to follow your heart.

26/04/04

hopeless romantic

As he searches for meaning to it all
She was right there offering the answers with open arms to him,
he couldn't realize he had been touched by an angel with love.

26/04/04

knights gambit

Certainly the way you move reminds me of a carefully planned out Check
Mate strategy,
Every slight move has its exact purpose,
One move after another played out in perfect Symmetry,
The move has been made and I'm waiting for the reaction,
It's played out Check Mate in 1,
The sacrifice has been made but I know it has been a fruitless attempt,
Really there was no attempt made,
The time spent playing the Game is all I can live for,
Like when sailing to discover new shore, when nothing appears on the
horizon I just accept it but sail for more.

26/04/04

is media the message?

The question that plagues all of society and then makes wealth a necessity,
We are called to play the audience to whatever is dictated no matter its
source or origins,
Our minds seem to work best under command, instruction, or need, but in
the end it all comes down to want,
What we want or who we want occupies the majority of hours,
We have not yet come to terms with our very own existence although we try
to mask that fact,
I'm afraid to notice that our world is out of whack,

Is it just our actions trying to keep pace with our technology?
Or is it our relentless advancements trying to dictate our actions?
Our own minds lead towards our demise and like a dry sponge we absorb
anything without question,
It's all about the false images we interrupt and believe without fully
comprehending the message,
The wrong messages are being dispersed by cynical Media with even scarier
producers,
The very few people in control will only get stronger making their product
something more powerful than air,
We breathe whatever's in abundance and available without a care,

Our creations will be our downfall,
Through overpopulation and hence pollution we create a fish bowl with more
fish than water can support,
What we see on the big screen or on our TVs is the Media and you are
responsible to decode its message,
Media has no power over you when you use your mind to understand your
own message,

Everything old had its time and knowing how it unfolded should guide us to a future not an end,
Who can we turn to for leadership and why does its power lead to corruption?
Belonging to something where the message you support is furthered is a way to exist,
The mind never stops when constantly challenged and this is a way to keep busy,
What you do is break away from the regular to keep the synapses firing and encourage new growth,

Our creations will be our downfall,
Through overpopulation and hence pollution we create a fish bowl with more fish than water can support,
What we see on the big screen or on our TVs is the Media and you are responsible to decode its message,
Media has no power over you when you use your mind to understand your own message,

07/05/05

great provider

To the one who holds authority and demonstrates it with utmost care,
You who deserve to have everything that can be desired and holds much to
be admired, enticing others to stare,
To go against your will would be blasphemy,
And to live by it would mean to understand complete ecstasy,

Because what you say goes without a doubt and harnesses more respect than
a boy scout,
The uncanny ability to play Puppet Master has become a synch,
With the valuable life lessons you have provided you have evoked gains in
miles while others only advance by the inch,
We once unsure of ourselves now react with certainty in all situations
because of great tutelage from you,
Like the gardener who planted seeds you can watch your children grow and
we all owe so much to you for everything we can do,

Having been repotted you've hoisted our pots high to where the sun shines
bright,
Because of you we can now take on any challenge with confidence knowing
we have already won the fight.

28/04/05

feeling alive

Hear me,
Talk to me,
Listen to me,
I don't care, even yell at me!

All of these events prove I'm Alive,
Even after going through the Mill I still need to feel like I've survived.
It might not always seem fair but the truth is,
You don't get given anything that you can't deal with,
Try to find the positive hidden within the ordeal,
It is there, you may just have to look a little, be patient,
Simply by communicating with others, and the wrapping paper has come off,
Listen to me my friend,
Just by interacting with something you don't understand you've proven what
you're trying to realize,
By communicating with something you prove that you are Alive.

02/03/03

fear of pain

Why do we attempt to rid our lives of pain,
when pain is sometimes the only thing that is truly real?
How do we bamboozle pain to escape it and not endure its valuable lessons?
Who represents the authority trying to play the true higher power?
What seems to be society's answer for anything that tricks the mind into
submission?
The pill, the drink, the cigarette, the narcotic, these are the things that
embrace an aura that is psychotic,
The only answer we supply to almost everything is the fogging of our senses
with a drug which is the answer furthest from heroic,

We were meant to feel pain and suffer sadness,
To overcome these afflictions the necessary recourse is found in the power of
the mind,
It isn't only wrong to take part in these games; it is sometimes a path right to
the wrong side,
Like the emotions evoked by being caught red handed when you can smell
guilt in the air,
Feeling like you need a drag or a drink; maybe a line or a pill; what you need
to do is think,
These cop-outs lead to energy's abyss and leave you searching for answers,
These resolutions will never become apparent while your mind is being
influenced,
The happiness you seek is all around; you must feel it not needing for it to be
induced,

To be truly content the only course of action is indwelling,
You must find the embodiment of joy in the most simple of circumstances,
Something that money or wealth cannot even attempt to buy,
Trying to purchase happiness and security is almost like selling your soul to
the Devil,
It is all in the choices we make and the lives affected by these,
By choosing not to affect other but changing your tune to support what is
good you can alleviate the need for endorphins,
You place your faith in the production of Serotonin and realize you control
its production by how you view the world,

If you can't change your circumstances, try changing your perspective;
It is the only way to truly live,
And this is achieved not through what you take but what you give,

06/23/05

every castle

Every castle, like the sun, goes down,
When you try to fight it, people ask, "Why cause yourself to frown? "
There's nothing you can do about it so why worry?
You have to remember there ain't no hurry,
The fortune teller lied,
It wasn't meant to happen, if it was it would!
The feeling was so real
It's true that in the pit of my stomach I still feel.

Sweet Love vanishes like a shadow in the morning,
The loss you feel just like trying to swallow the large pill,
But remember when it goes down it's just like turning the page, a fresh
beginning.

The construction of a new castle begins,
It may take awhile, but you know the paradise you reach will be well worth
the wait.
When I dream I still see the castle,
I once dreamt about past castles, only now I've got my sights set on the space
station.

12/06/03

cyclic change

Everything seems to move in cycles that repeat themselves quite regularly,
Like the pay-out programmed into a slot machine or the perfect poker hand,
Earth quakes, hurricanes, and even tsunamis move in occurrence with
accuracy characteristic of a Swiss watch,
The thing that has baffled human existence is the understanding of how to
read these hiccups of nature,
We humans have mastered nearly all in our world and in doing so have
caused Mother Nature to decide to play unfairly,

With that pollution our inventions produce we are like the painter who has
painted himself into a corner,
As technology becomes futuristic, markets become global,
Our minds still don't understand that every little thing we do has a
consequence whether good or bad,
Upon realization of our mistakes we will be left in the corner with no option
but like Citizen Kane to shriek, "The Horror! The Horror!"

It is not too late to stop the cycle and in doing so change our fate,
A simple change in the way we think will lead to colossal differences in our
very existence,
To move from the "Want" attitude to what is essentially "Needed" could
prove to be the S.O.S that is becoming plain to see,
This change in moral is becoming a necessity leaving little time to ponder its
obvious our survival depends on it and we haven't got time to waste,

Immediacy related to the media is putting the cart before the horse and if
you think about it showing us too much,
We are left believing what we see on the screen and have no choice but to
play along,
Hollywood may in fact be the nexus of the universe perhaps where the forces
of evil reside,
We need a strong Soul to model ourselves after; to live like; to be like as such,

How long do we have to wait to see another mortal like Jesus Christ or an existence as clever,
What the world needs now is love, it is something there is just too little of,
When Tybalt was fighting with Romeo the words revealed could be our savior,
"Be Satisfied! Be Satisfied!" is the advancement we all must achieve,
It is the only way in this world we can survive and perhaps our existence will gain a rightful place, being present forever,

03/04/05

the realization

Like tuning a violin you educated my soul,
With your beauty you brought attention,
To ensure your comfort I played tough,
Only to cause smiles forever was my goal,

The pleasure was all mine,
At this moment the words are hard to find,
Understanding the emotion is simple,
I have felt it before but never so fine,

Linguistic determinism is language controlling thought,
Cognito ergo sum,
In Italia e vero che ti amo,
Per sempre e sempre sono vero,

Smile for me now,
Sei veramente bella,
Anything for you,
You really are wow!

17/9/06

volume two:
"inspirations"

embodying beauty

The notion of encapsulating beauty is vast, yet very specific.
Like catching a firefly in a bottle where its warm glow can be hypnotic.
A similar trance can be experienced being in the same place as beauty.
It can be experienced in a fraction of a second with its affects lasting
indefinitely.
Once beauty has been determined to exist an aura is noticed existing around
the entity.
When beauty is confirmed its radiant shimmer is available for all to see.

How does beauty truly exist?
Is it in sight of the eye, or sight of the mind, or sight of the heart?
Can the mind see? Can the heart copy the ability of the eye?
Does energy exist in what is beautiful?
When does beauty show itself with all its wonder and mystery?

Answers to these questions and every query are available when beauty is
believed triumphant in every scenario.
This occurs when a soul is realized to be a reality in every single thing.
Beauty is not in the "show" but in what is withheld from view and
understanding.
True beauty does exist however the trick is to find it.
When found this trick metamorphoses to being near it as much as possible.
And this dear friends is the embodiment of beauty,

This monumental event of embodying beauty only occurs when souls unite.
Like fitting puzzle pieces together as if the connections were air tight.
When true beauty is found magically the fireworks and sparklers ignite.
True beauty is an awesome sight and once found nothing will seem more
right.

08/02/08

you inspire

You instill in me what I have always dreamt of feeling,
Now my ship has sailed, and you are the destination,
Will I be King?
Will you be Queen?
As the most valuable player you hold all the cards,
Your judgment dictates the course of the game,
As a pawn to move across the field you have always been the goal,
When pawn converts to queen the energy produced is eternal,
My love for you is eternal,
You can not lose,
This love is certain; infinity + 1,

18/07/07

why do hearts ache?

Intolerable emotion winds its way through my veins draining me of all vigor,
It's been six days and now six nights my mind works continuously,
Employed with the task of discerning what went wrong while facing each sunrise,
Understanding the situation leaves me more enraged and desperate for something,
But it is something that ruined us.

Waiting to see our future in your eyes is a moment I anticipate,
Needing to wait for that is unbearable and concentration is a complicated endeavor,
How such real emotions can hurt so much is baffling and not comprehensible,
Something that is, should not be, and no matter what is said, the addiction rules.
The pain is like what is felt during a nightmare where everything scares.

Things that could have been done differently are like grains of sand on a Caribbean beach,
What is done is done and what has ended should stay ended,
Hearts ache because they are meant to and this allows you to become stronger and wiser,
However the pain accompanies a lesson that is unfortunately a necessity to learn,
This lesson is about yourself.

Realizing the sincerity of your heart is a frightening ordeal that should not be faced alone,
But alone it must be faced and learned as to prevent the lesson from being repeated again,
The degree of ache in your heart measures the purity of the lesson meant for you to learn,
Real lessons numb your mind while consciousness continues and the hurt left behind,
If granted one wish it would be to rewind.

23/09/07

belief

Having a belief is something magical,
Having a want may be cynical,
Having a desire is fulfilling your destiny,

Wanting is sometimes pure,
Living requires a soul to endure,
When emotion is this real it is something sure,

When the days turn into months the spirit establishes,
When day turns to night satisfied are all my wishes,
My soul, my spirit, my heart now has its goal,
To exist hand in hand; two bodies sharing one soul,

26/07/07

reasons

The reasons have become more real than pure water,
For these reasons my eyes have been opened,
Each reason can be answered by one word,

Love makes sense to suffocate you with,
My heart is in you 100%,
Every answer stems from your encompassing energy,
Every breath comes from you; my soul is tangled in your life,

Enjoying you, being with you, Loving you, pleases my dreams,
You are my dreams, my angel,

14/08/07

feelings once upon a time

If this is life then I accept it,
I embrace it,
I embrace you.

Everything about you has me anticipating the next page,
The next page of the never ending story.
Everything you have gone through leaves me feeling compassion,
Compassion rolled in warm passion.
It's like a "piggy in a blanket" where you are the warm meat wrapped gently
in my arms. Hear it, believe it, "Under my Arm Forever, ever, ..."

I look forward to a life with You, Emma, Elvis,
All about synapse growth to exist hand in hand on the same page,
To play with your energy so delicately,
In you exists all the knowledge of the sage,
Truly you compliment and are the one, the only.

22/07/07

miracle worker

As time goes by the miracle materializes,
Upon every meeting synapses are awakened,
Through your cherished effort my body responds like a trained animal to its command,
With every passing moment the emotion deep within crystallizes,

Like an empty basin I eagerly await to be replenished with your eternity of knowledge,
It is not only in your instruction that I am blessed,
The energy level that surrounds you like a force field is fed upon,
I feel that energy with every embrace and want to be lost there,
Most never acquire the level of understanding you exhibit,

It is in these arms which you have given life that I now exhibit my own knowledge,
You deserve the world and by understanding this you in turn share the world with others,
Once my life was on a one way road that led to a dead end,
Now I can turn the next page in the never ending story and I want you to know that without your love I couldn't ever mend,
You will never be forgotten and will always be loved.

08/17/06

keylynn lorain

A normal day turned extraordinary with a single encounter,
A normal Friday entails tardiness however being responsible entails
structured authority,
Flowers enjoy energy from the sun,
Automobiles enjoy energy stored in their fuel,
I enjoyed the energy I felt during the simple act of being around her,

It was a chance meeting that revolutionized my understanding of meaning,
What works like a double edged sword acts both as friend and foe,
 This weapon can make a life euphoric or can take a soul through torture,
It is your very own mind,

The words spouted from my mouth like the water out of a fountain at a park,
On this day my thoughts were put into words that echoed with majesty deep
within me,
With the Jazzy backdrop of uptown Waterloo the air provoked an abyss of
thought,
The feeling of complete satisfaction would suffocate me with the most
pleasant emotion,
Similar to the satisfaction a child feels when the light goes on if he's afraid of
the dark,

With fascination I watched poetry in motion in her lips with every grin,
With the glow of an Angel she moved slowly around me confidence was
always building,
Inspiration comes standard in meetings like this but on this night it was
extremely potent,
Free walking came back to me this night and with confidence I maintained
balance,
Miraculous and surprising to me I anticipate the next meetings,
And look forward for this relationship to begin,

If the bud is to bloom many cells must hear their call,
I can see her spirit through her eyes as they are windows to her soul,
I want to disclose everything to this flower that has been revealed to me,
I notice the sparkle in her eyes with the rose in her cheeks,
The energy is addictive and after all she could be a Wonderwall,

7/07/06

exhilaration

Understanding of emotion related is sometimes welcomed and sometimes dreaded,
If the catalyst is sentimentally desirable; euphoric, traumatic palpitations of the heart materialize,
When such a catalyst defies wisdom, choosing to exist where light is not welcome; the affair shivers,
Mental state, like the centurion, promotes justice and good will,
However demons' demise formulates notion when fear with darkness is embedded,

Like the acceleration of what is finely tuned the positive catalyst leaves twelve singing pistons,
Meanwhile what lacks creative beauty is a let down like gasping for air when oxygen is deceased,
Before enduring negative exhilaration the soul itself is found to quiver,
Catching glimpse of what beauty leads here,
So to witness the departure of the soul through teary eyes exhilaration is guilty,
Accompanying sorrow endorphins face annihilation with tears being shed.

What is felt in all purity depends pivotally within motive realized,
Knowing intention like the reunion of lost souls leads to demagnification of beauty,
Finding the catalyst to your exhilaration is referred to by the divine mystics within mind,
The catalyst being additive leaves involvement to interpretation open,
In gorgeous eyes perhaps catalytic conversion are the directions to heaven,

11/02/08

can you

Can you believe it? can you comprehend?
It's straight forward to me; this road leads to the end,
For all time the road has been the symbol of accomplishment and now is
what takes me to satisfaction,
It's comforting to me to not know what's around the bend;
just being sure it's a "Good Thing."

Things are what fill every moment of every day but you are the thing that
makes me feel like a King,
King of the castle is the knowledgeable understanding I draw from you,
Like the osmosis of water drawing the molecules into the air,
The draw the magnet has over an unsuspecting metallic object is like the
attraction you hold over me,
All these analogies are my way of inviting you to understand everything you
mean to me,
In an eight day week you have built the temple in 3 days,
What was a ruin is now a palace in Utopia where the only emotion felt is
Euphoria.

Can you fathom the turn of events?
Can you understand?
Can you see how your key fits my lock?
Like a shepherd I will tend to you and the flock,
Where the life of the little lamb takes precedence over my own,
I feel this all for you for the love you have already shown,

02/07/07

chivalry dead

This notion of heroics has deceased but only its reception has lost true understanding,
Kindness today goes misunderstood leaving ulterior motives to be inferred,
In what lacks true intention is substituted for the reality of a bad dream,
Where persons experience only what plays looped continuously behind the eyelid,

The frustration associated with knowing it is true inspires emptiness of emotion,
Where emotion acts like the bully inviting punishment,
Only real punishment is when emotions cease to exist,
Now only remorse exists in the mind and the exhale of submission surrounds the soul,
All sublimations amount to a conception of the mind reminding she was only a kid,

Reality proves souls are lost crusaders along the path that ends in continual needing,
A life defies purpose when the struggle to obtain has been premature in its cognition,
Where thinking leads cognition is afraid to follow,
Like the leashed dog whose route is predetermined chivalry can not exist in these times,

16/02/08

true exhilarations

After the evening submerged in endorphins the mind is truly satisfied,
Finding out remarkable events take your mind through the labyrinth is overwhelming,
Seeing the beauty in what you thought was lost brings back memories of what is novel,
Being on the back of the mountain brings three down the Front,
Being in close proximity to the monster keeps nerve endings sensitive to the emotion,
Finally tackling the monster precludes a boot-lift,
With the soldier at attention possibility opens the door,

After guiding the bucket down the front the bowl of sugar is the stranger at the gate,
Before the realization of the feat actually exits the mind is at peace,
Like a silence before the storm tethers are strained while injured eyes inexplicably wide,
How this situation leaves possibility balanced with the unforeseen weight of divinity,
Pure exhilaration is made true by the plunder into the sugar fermented in the bowl,
Without the satisfaction of an inhale the journey completed,
On the last day repercussions can not squander the mood,

An easy ride leads to the Camel's hump where to exist in euphoric wonder is inviting,
One more Easy ride completes exhilaration like a spark completes ignition,
Straight into the chalet facilitates anticipation,
With what is something sure he waits for the unveiling of familiarity,
Knowing that completion is achieved in a single bite the gate to the esophagus is opened,
Wait for it! wait for it! the moment is upon you; penetrating darkness signals the exhale,
Glands vomit with satisfaction as completion of a monumental event occurs,
It is but a fairy tale and we all venture to live happily ever after,

11/03/08

overanxious

The way the mind coaxes to action is sometimes ill-suited for a given situation,
It's confusing logic at one moment that was mistakenly premature,
What it is that inspires such action is in all truthfulness a mystery,
If only it was possible to know the outcome of actions prior to their performance,
If only actions that concluded in heart aches or negative consequence were retired before occurrence,
Problems that never occur are never solved by sitting on the fence,

The secret to a rebuttal lies in calculated and patient thought,
When the marble finds its way through the series of columns the glee is seen in a child's eyes,
In the hopes of playing the audience to such a feat many avenues are explored,
Taking the vehicle down the alley that ends abruptly is no better than a bucket with a hole,
Over anxiousness is like excitement attributed to a game winning goal,
Followed by the whistle and notification from officials that it does not count,

Having to absorb these feelings of dismay very often frustrates,
To send any recollection tonight is purposeless for it is too late,
This avenue will only bear fruit if patience can convince this meeting was fate,

20/03/08

poetic mastery

A place where light and darkness exist as one is where this unachievable
notion resides,
The place where true talent is common and communication is found almost
lyrical,
Putting words together as an art relies on an empty mind full of possibility,
It is cognitive wonder where word selection makes its triumphant novelty a
reality,
The poet's thoughts imprisoned on the page awaiting inquisitive eyes to decide,

The fate of the word written relies solely on its interpretation,
Left hanging delicately in the balance of literary genius and what creates the
mausoleum,
When power is interred with wisdom meaning cries to be understood,
Author deems appropriate assignment of understanding for what may not be
understood,
In the fine balance present under the wing of the sparrow mastery can be
witnessed,
If only poetic exchange is substituted for common interaction the porthole opens,
Looking in, similar to realizing Pandora's Box allows realistic understanding,
Its mystery, surrounded by wonder, holds keys that unlock endorphin release,
Pursuing Mastery is like causing reaction, leaving encrypted invisible ink in
the nude,
Without wardrobe is the way to be purely viewed,

The inspiration from such an event is true,
Leaving the mind gasping for relief while the parasympathetic system is on
sabbatical,
Through the eye the image encoded will forever exist,
See the embodiment of beauty just out of reach,
These emotions released leave completion just out of reach,

03/04/08

noticing

Noticing the cues that have been left for you to see is something inspiring,
The true wonder becomes evident when you make that connection between notes,
Like filling in the melody to the song and knowing the record is almost produced,
Like completing the Manuscript and believing in publication; these cognitions do inspire,

Not only does the mind approach self-actualization,
The entire body rejoices in the knowledge of accomplishment,
Little nuances are meant to motivate while these signs are intrigued by the vision,
Little do society's inspectors value in the realm of energy awareness,

Need for understanding is necessary to realize this next evolution of mind,
Truly our civilization must open our minds to such a possibility,
Leaving the mind closed to the road signs meant to be followed also leaves souls in peril,
Lacking the foresight to navigate the route is a life spent in confusion,

Near to the sign is where keys to salvation were left,
To unlock the gate the skeleton key is a necessity,
Looking for that key is accepting the unquenchable thirst,
Leaving the key hidden could mean the conclusion to humanity,

Noticing the shimmer of light reflected leaves its witness in complete omnipotence,
To manifest such an awakening leaves the mind open to stupefied sincerity,
Launching powers endowed leaves the hypothalamus struggling to produce its offspring,
Loving your existence allows free flowing radicals to infiltrate both mind and heart,

08/03/08

pondering retribution

A place where imagination is in control while its products demand careful
attention,
The way the mind opens like the blossom of a tulip inspires further
excavation,
Careful analysis of cognitive treasures to be unwrapped unleashes a
thunderstorm of emotion,
Bringing about satisfaction leaves nothing to bud paranoia and keeps
insanity at the gates of the mansion,

Microwaves promote molecular vibrations of the magical bond between
hydrogen and oxygen,
The water particles shake with velocities unimaginable and rarely even seen,
A metamorphosis into steam prescribes volume increase and corn is
transformed through a process unseen
Now awaiting garnish while expelling the last of the moisture trapped within,

It is in this location that equality thrives leaving no room for comparison,
It's where energy is funneled through the skull and into the brain,
Understanding and compassion make their mark noticeably seen,
To receive positive feedback leaves the grimiest of villain feeling clean.

22/03/08

silhouettes generate cognition

In a mind's eye a figure is appraised,
The sight of which leaves the mind, hart, and soul amazed,
Beauty in the eye registers with ease in a brain,
Thoughts to incorporate such delicate wonder into daily witness are a
welcomed pain,
Like a breath taking flower upon its bloom is the energy felt whenever she
enters a room,

How such does unbridled sexuality manifest in the shadows of the mind?
Do eyes communicate with the heart which then expresses itself through the
oral cavity?
Can she read the encoded message of mine?

With familiarity tender eyes look for the sign,
Like the tennis ball returned after service the energy completes the circle
from her to me,
Perhaps the equation will not balance or leave in frustration what should be
divine,

Poetic verse leaves open the mind for interpretation,
To uncover riddles your mind holds against you is something euphoric,
It is in the mystery of the woman where possibility lies to recycle the nation,
It is patience men must befriend to rescue their hearts and prove they are
heroic,
What could be something to ignore is the same thing that gives a heart
permission to soar,

15/03/08

the absence

The absence of, and therefore its lack, both mentally and physically drain vitality,
The mind works to sabotage your existence as the body responds to the mind's instruction,
Like corporals to their sergeant the mind commands and the body obeys,
Who is in control of the ship?

Tribulations not resolved invite comparison and leave to chance the solution to the riddle,
A chance to witness true exhilarating power lies in the ripples of the dormant mind,
Without this energy working to make homeostasis in every clause, malevolence is furthered along its way,
How can benevolence triumph when the relationship is irrecoverable and the kiss has left the lip,

Absence of the energy holds the stomach in disarray while nauseating sensations infiltrate the coliseum,
Death brings the absence of bodily awareness; meanwhile, the soul lives on,
It is the soul that we put through the training to vibrate with oscillations equivalent to time travel,
When can the understanding of this absence be realized and the antonym to absence emerge?

The realization is internal while you must choose to be the captain in your life,
From lip to lip the perfect communication is made and euphoria is close,
To only decide is left while full knowledge of the power you possess can be stabilizing,
This absence is waiting for the key to unlock the door and the key is in the adventure that comes with you,

21/03/08

the oracle transpires reality

Reality is the force that kills,
For a close friend reality is marvelous,
Knowing that a relationship is precious is a demand to be cautious,
Finding trust can be like finding a diamond on the beach amidst the sand,
Noticing energy sparkle in lovers' eyes symbolizes the oracle is present,
People may ask but it's hard to say where she went,
Hearts can mend but taking one's life in suicide is the end,
Is the oracle in you to protect?
Use it to maximize the potency of your affect,
Satisfaction is overwhelming when energy transfer is complete,
When it struggles to happen bottled up energy suffocates,
The weary traveler is left empty handed at the gates.

20/03/08

unobstructed vision

The truth is, perception can occur without awareness,
Achieved through careful understanding, vision becomes apparent,
Something that is not yet fully understood lurks in the shadows, patiently waiting for approval,
Like the new kid at recess who keeps his eyes low; meanwhile, waiting patiently to join,
Noticing the others frolic around full of calculated carelessness.

Cones and rods fill the visual receptors behind the eye,
Through the cornea the pupil chooses to focus light on the retina,
The precision of this embodiment determines clarity,
But true clarity is found only with the understanding,
Do not take for granted the fact reality may lie.

Circumvallate papillae and foliate papillae ensure taste.
Is it what light carries that ensures vision?
Could it be synapses revealing truth that allow for sight?
Feeling energy transfer for which real vision accounts,
Other theories have yet to be denounced.

Complete rejection of scientific proofs is all together idiotic,
Today's education and learning methods are all too systematic,
This realization will eventually be greeted by the Master of the Universe,
Reestablishing everyday cognitions of the next generation before unveiled,
Seeing the possibility for change is the need before realizing we have failed.

24/03/08

mind power

All that is of vital importance is what can be found to the left of the right ear,
It is a never ending battle to always be on the defensive while having
negative thoughts to fear,
In relation to such thoughts that bombard with negativity it is the brain's duty
to goal tend,
To keep stable, to keep positive, to keep content, living in the position of
authority every year,

A strong mind needs its exercise to remain both cognitively and physically fit,
Achieved through authentic thought the mind's exercise is delivered,
Like the exercise fanatic who genuinely enjoys the experience of tormenting
the body,
This mind knows well full satisfaction occurs only following a mental strain
delivering the hit,

Believe in something noble while maintaining conscious awareness of life,
Only the mind possesses the ability to signal the parasympathetic nervous
system,
Mobilizing necessary endorphins that when called to duty alter reality,
Before mental security can happen choose to see through angelic eyes,
This transition's the step towards inspirational thought and never dies.

25/03/08

security gives birth to stability

Through discussion security is achieved which in turn produces stability,
The principals of group awareness are primarily concerned with perception,
It is perceptions that are the primary force in guiding a soul's way through life,
What is deduced from personal perception is like the vote that alters the
scale in favor of accomplishment,

The perceptions of foreign eyes can be detrimental and invalidate stability
which prevents security,
The perceptions believed by personal eyes may also lead to similar results,
Learning not every opinion deserves acceptance reveals new attitudes of
fortitude,
Like an unbearable fallacy committed where the only option is to repent,

The erroneous belief is equivalent to the misleading notion that incriminates
possibility,
Like decoding the encrypted love letter slid under the door by someone alien,
With not so much as a word, knowledge is bestowed upon whoever comes,
Stability is robbed from whoever realizes their draft of the terminating letter
is already sent,

Security found in the puddle is tormenting conclusively
Stability can be achieved when molecular motion is halted and the puddle
now frozen,
Leaving myth classified as a subjective contour whose form is not known,
Little anxieties are attributed to imagination concerning what is beneath the tent,

Being secure in the chosen regime builds of mortar society's stability,
Realizing power is derived from what is stable prepares society for the monsoon,
Being faithful in everyday routine solidifies security which in turn promotes
a divinity,
Security fundamentally ensures stability to which entire civilizations are left
to augment,

27/03/08

a b c's for u

As the coaster pulls back into the station emotions take the field,
An ever changing circuit like a Rubix Cube must be rebuilt,
All gifts have a selfish quality evident with desired reciprocity,
Angels deliver what lacks in the human mind trapped in the city

Beautiful like the flower's seed your beauty will develop like the sunshine,
Before light of day it is you who make figure eights in my mind,
Behind closed doors the mystery can be read in full,
Be it from the depth of the universe on my heart you pull,

Clutching love tightly muscles are exhausted,
Clear windshields guarantee vision albeit vision can never be trusted,
Clover makes sight improved while dealing with romance,
Clean consciousness welcomes inspiring hearts to beat and then dance,

31/03/08

is truth dead?

The notion of truth should be something eternal,
Even happiness is only real when shared,
The constraints of life attempt to make truth not true,
Children learn truth as lies in media when truth's fragility is only up to you,

The way you move causes fragility in my heart with a tongue of knots,
A knot ties us together with the love for an art of linguistic expression,
What do you see while you dream?
All thoughts are dedications to you while endorphins flood my soul,
Knowing that comfortable energy is forever the goal,

To you truth can be the foundation on which to build what might come,
That sparkle that reflects in your eyes encourages synaptic pleasures,
Too many minutes elapse before again you are able to deliver your smile,
To never speak lies means truth is alive in what was thought to be dust,
Confidence in what the knot stands for is something forever to trust,

This truth can live forever,
Upon which it may be called whenever,
Truth is alive and it will survive in every weather.

03/04/08

distance

The distance by no means a journey yet is for now not to be taken lightly,
In a New York minute activity is feverish as minds search for completion,
Can satisfaction be balanced with desire or is this mission forfeited?

The secret to the riddle lies waiting to be unveiled,
Like the bride on her wedding day waits for the veil to be lifted as forever is,
Sealed with the meeting of lips under heaven's permission the kiss completes,

The treasure has been found in the mystery and the distance now measured,
In the mission of romantic understanding the gates remain barred to finding,
What can not be found waits in comfort while maturing like a fine wine,

Ready for peace to finally gain control marks the distance as flowers do a path,
Peace delivered in the presence of a flower attributes emotions' bounty for you,
Completion is finding you when the distance has been surpassed.

04/04/08

that one

That one that harmonizes your soul is who you were put here to find,
From right under your nose the angel appeared just over the left shoulder,
That distance between so little yet never explored,
To spend time playing the game is in the forecast of will,

Enjoying sunrise after sunset emotion furthers the immaculate relationship
as it gains substance,
In conversation words are exchanged; however, energy transfer is the one
magical quality of love,
Without respect the mystery drains all emotion from above,
Respecting the belief makes the joy of life resemble you,

Keeping your mind calm while fantastic realizations intrude lets serenity exist,
Cognition will go inlayed with careful navigation while actions are delayed,
While the earth encircles the sun an aura of pure beauty suffocates the heart,
As the sun again rises dew and grass are to marry,

The question posed does not require response but is inspiring for consideration,
The game is played with the mouth closed as transmissions are completed
from heart to heart,
Only the angel possesses the knowledge sought to end a solitary lifestyle,
When psychology ends the bonds will still exist between you and me,

05/04/08

train motion

The rhythmic motion sways sleep upon the innocent,
Visions appear in the mind's eye,
It is not this eye but the mind that sees and knows all,

We live in a sick society that capitalizes on immediacy,
The power of illusion often plays in competition with the power of the mind,
There is truth in dreams only their logic reminds of the prank call

Like the night terror of running down the endless hall,
Self sufficiency opens the realm of the possibility,
Strengthened spirituality encourages chance to challenge the fall,

Remembrance is plagued by subjective opinions,
When emotional stability relieves mental anguish your hand is secure,
That hand that does not judge promotes serendipity to serve,

To search for what inspires builds the mystery,
We are all working to build the mystery and make sense of our time here,
From a place where understanding is found in dependence; the choice is yours,

07/04/08

defining cool

Like Cool Man!
Put your coat on Nick it is kind of cool out,
Are you cool with that?
It's cool with me,
Your actions tonight can only be described as "Way Cool",

Context makes up the majority of the essence behind what is said,
Differing circumstances energize; contrasting synapses fire, giving
understanding,
Living examples of this reality can be found in a child's head,
Where novel words are born while everything heard invites new dialect,

The future is secure in an innocent mind,
Their choices easily made while security is effortless to find,
Through the eyes of a child mortality will survive,
This is cool knowing that this fact can allow humanity to stay alive,

Before people's insecurities can deny what is cool,
Bombast a definition to the word where its concept is to be defined,
Biased opinions of meaning betray what must be lived to comprehend,
Bending its meaning to suit is like a precious stone to be mined,

In words that challenge discernment communication can be omnipotent,
Ideologies surrounding what should be erudite sometimes inspire frustration,
Ignominious teachers need to retire instead of fondling their egos,
Ignorant to the ability to teach is in all truth not cool but that's the way life goes,

08/04/08

e-ma-ho

From a people so high, in reality, their country crests the heavens,
Tibetan words carry the essence that characterizes meaning,
By capturing emotion in syllabic sound *e-ma-ho* generates understanding of
sensation,
Meaning what is untranslatable to English *e-ma-ho* encompasses wonder and
awe,
Wonder and awe that is realized by truly coming to know reality,

Enigmatic reality is achieved by knowing you,
What can only be described as the blissful experience of knowing reality is
now good,

Like the Tibetan who matures to experiences *e-ma-ho*
Acknowledgement of this attainment is due to that aura which is you,
Loving life contributes to *e-ma-ho* while loving you is the wonder and awe
that makes my reality,

10/04/08

nodi

Bringing two pieces together to form an unbreakable bond,
Encompasses the notion of a knot,
Coming from the Latin *nodus* the node is where lives cross,
Also called a node this part on a plant is where leaves begin their growth,

Italian society works with nodi being where the relationship dawned,
Nodi are the ties that connect as knots bind loose yarn,
Originally referring to blood ties, moral affiliations belonged to the family,
Ordinary knots are untied every day but certain knots seem strong,

Two lives cross at the node,
When crossing inspires growth their futures remain untold,
Anticipated beautification of a relationship is waiting to unfold,
Looking for the one occurrence on which we hold,
Quando nodi seranno forte siamo bona bona,

11/04/08

sympathetic yet pragmatic

Sympathy awakened hearing your narration but dealing with the situation
must be done pragmatically,
In a sensible and realistic way the actions to follow must ensure survival,
At six in the morning thoughts begin their marathon through my mind,
When dealing with family sympathy runs strong near the front of the line,

Pragmatic thinking is always waiting in sympathy's blind spot and plays in
sympathy's mirrors,
Sympathy does not understand the depth of the hole while initial intentions
are to jump in,
The aftermath of the conversation left synapses engaged in a game of wits
all night,
Trying to balance sympathy with pragmatic intention exhausted the mental
stores ending in fright,

How can such personal intentions be left to decompose while maintaining
the bond?
Do realizations of invective language muscle their way to the front or is their
place in darkness?
What cognitions avenued thoughts to make such a request?
When did knowledge suffer as vanity left your chest?

It does not feel advantageous to participate in this merger when vitality
hangs in the balance,
Thinking is impaired by want which is governed by need for what is not
realistic to have,
Robbing the relationship of innocence is the product of this craving
disguised as a business transaction,
Wanting and needing are different trains of thought previewing elation,

Like a ship lost at sea every direction seems to replicate a mirror image,
Or like the innocent cheetah hunted for his spots and now kept in a cage,
Within the mass of fibrous tissues forsaking the mind, introspections now rage,
This predicament now offers enough complications to plague the sage,

15/04/08

experiences

Experiences are all you have; that can not be repudiated,
While wealth, health, and relationships can all be recanted, repossessed,
Cognitive preparation allows experience to be converted to semantic memory,
Thus moving into pseudo-permanent Long Term Memory,

From dreams to reality certain experiences are the missing link to establish the chain,
That puzzle piece not included in the prison of cardboard,
Like the diversity of colours exhibited in abstract art, experience humbles deviation,
While the sheer multitude of stars in the sky, commensurate amenities to see,

Significance of each memory depends primarily on context during its encoding,
In lucid prose, secrets to build a life on such experience leave emotions thunderstruck,
When two equal one all sagacities are heightened to a level of divinity,
Adventures exist behind the closed door and deciding to open it spells possibility,

Knowing this experience spells adventure fundamentally vibrates emotion,
An adventure to open the eyes to harmony existing unpainted on the canvas,
An artist only knows the exact coordinates the brush must be in union with,
Like lips in union with their reflection on another face, both are full of glee,

Such an experience companies illumination of enlightenment,
Variegated with wonder and anxiety this experience opens the impassible gates,
Knowing this experience obscurely promotes the next chapter encouraging ramification,
What can be classified as a peremptory life, this experience can be the hyperbole deed,

17/04/08

true contentment

True contentment lies in what is unexplainable,
Vibrating in harmony with expectation leaves souls expecting perfect
remittance,
In what inspires the next heart beat promotes answers,
While what is true makes dreams equated with reality,

Tautology of her words exist forever in the head,
And their significant message remains untold,
Melodious harps sing sweet lullabies as rest is anticipated,
Effortless conversions of pain to love existed while he waited,

Temptations to speak love seduce the vocal cords but in silence they remain,
Waiting for reciprocity allows intentions to crystallize,
Keeping enchantment alive in a heart allows purity's dispersion,
Retention of faith bleeds contentment from seclusion,

Testimonies of truths generate relationship's bonds,
When contentment is found in what is true life is then actualized,
Drastic measures are required for this to occur,
But when complete amazing satisfaction is now for sure,

17/04/08

the choice

Choices govern all,
Healthiness is a choice,
Safety is a choice,
Relationships are choices.
Like the brown bag theory-what comes out of the bag must have been put in,
Rapaciousness attempts to assume control of the choice and must be
disciplined,

Dictatorial will power controls actions and thoughts through choices,
Emancipation of desire leads to prosperous choosing throughout the day,
While bestowing attention to what the mind covets furnishes a reality with fear,
Similar to not expecting what is reflected in the mirror,

Good choices preclude every smile and leave open the possibility for
reiteration,
Recapitulation of the energy experienced while encountering a smile then
comes,
Life hangs in the balance that pivotally depends on the choice,
All choices are up to your angelic body with your outstanding voice,

18/04/08

in the morning

During the time of regenerated curiosity ideas spawn from the void that fills,
Being in that state open to suggestibility stimulates what furthers the truth,
Keeping a faith true to the heart leaves possibility in control of personal mandate,
Faith reminds the soul that vivacity follows a line drawn by fate,

Believing in a life governed by faith reserves radiance's emotion to create,
Faith forges an astounding reality by your instruction like the medieval sword,
Shaped in fire then appointed by nobility it is this lustrous occasion that defines,
In the morning is found inspiration that makes the sun want to shine,

This inspiration balancing delicately before what civilization has chosen as King,
Spasmodic trains of thought are common without that energy that you bring,
Exuberance obtained in the morning ritual sufficiently engages an understanding,
A symbolic gesture of love forecast by the giving of a ring,

In time to discover that what has always been resides in Morning Prayer,
Comprehending the mystery along the path reminds us of the Method of Loci,
A walk through the forest allows a relationship to add another layer,
With eyes open the mystery is incomplete but with an open heart we truly see,

19/04/08

studying life & love

Living life while psychology's rules are against defines the mind trap,
Loving life regardless lets harmony vibrate next to the soul,
Accepting life for what it is invites endorphins' free flow,
Spending every moment enjoying a permanent smile is the goal,

The experience of this world is highly subjective which creates awe,
Along with wonder love just doesn't make any sense at all,
So some experience begs the question, "why in love, do we fall?"
Where does the heart exist when it has fallen into the black hole?

The potential for personal growth resides within reach,
Only to take that chance can lead to a satisfied existence,
Peril has no place in the sanctuary where trust sits showing patience,
Capitalizing on the situation means the end of long personal penance,

It is all up to that One who decides to return the call,
Amazement is found while deeper and deeper I fall,
Inspired to walk great lengths knowing your lips wait at the end of the hall,
It is with someone that I want to share it all,

21/04/08

needs in life

Security is all that need be strived for,
Finding satisfaction in what comes commonly reveals the secret to a life,
Too many live struggling for what they think they want,
While most wants are unsuited to fit the puzzle,
Like oil mixed with water such molecules can not find harmony,

Looking for what is wanted rarely partners with what is needed,
Realizing this truth confuses the insecure thus drains vitality,
Understanding genuine need makes the sages shed their mortality,
Abraham Maslow enlightens with his hierarchy of needs quite masterfully,

Physiological needs are required at the base of life itself and must be
satisfied,
Security then takes its stand encompassing long-term survival, bearing
stability,
All other needs and wants sit comfortably on this foundation now laid,
With this base the pyramid to self-actualization is constructed ultimately,

Security plays the lullaby necessary for cell rejuvenation,
Being secure guarantees the mind's ease,
This ease promotes self-help and leads to society's retribution,
In doing so security gives minds peace that will save every nation,

23/04/08

capturing insight

Being in the midst of the idea both energizes and complicates,
Answering the question supplements the voyage in search of truth,
Responding to the ultimate call should invigorate the youth,
Understanding insight brings power to lessons involving couth.

Hearing the message requests immediate action by leaving the routine,
Following your intension promotes composure rarely ever seen,
Knowing actions performed today are scheduled to unveil what is pristine,
Believing in the insight then fosters all things pure and clean,

From a purity reminiscent of a surgeon's sterilized environment,
The insight captured in the dream defies apathy to discover what is truly meant,
Leaving to record from memory leaves one sometimes unsure of how things went,
Capturing insight graduates the mind realizing it is something to us only lent.

24/04/08

family

A model to conform to,
Even if partially,
This support system superintends a budding life,
A life with so much possibility similar to the mound of moist clay,
The clay that needs turning to realize its certain potential,

With what may be achieved through observational learning is thus
conditioned,
Supernatural powers at work influence conventional thought
Providing miraculous propositions to Einstein, Pavlov, and Mozart,
The prescribed ideas facilitate existence while promoting the soul,
Such contributions satisfy proper steps towards the goal,

Realizing a goal so sublime invites clarity,
Yet this realization is achieved all too rarely,
Familiar bonds determine manumission from life's Herculean demands,
The family is worth every personality it evokes,
Dreams that energize the soul are what the family stokes,

The family guides personal aptitude,
Giving all decisions the algorithm for eminence,
Promptly substantiating the family's values establishes the rubric to live by,
Networking through the family will guarantee one to have their say,
But conformity in a family makes tomorrow's possibility today.

25/04/08

the apology

Can't lie but want to make things right,
Living with what's been done makes it difficult to sleep at night,
One thing you needed to understand is like the footprint left in the sand,
Erase itself from embarrassment is what the tide demands,

Seeing the fire extinguished makes the light die,
Frustrations play hide & seek in the hallways of my mind,
Like an echo resonating within, the only word to think is 'why?',
With the way things have happened it might be possible to cry,

If only to relive the situation things would change,
Anything to live through this part of life those evil forces arranged,
Breathing when there's no air is like not living the thoughts of adventures we shared,
Sorry to think that life got confused when it was thought I might have cared,

In the middle of night suffering to apologize torments the mind,
Impulse can be blamed for what's now true,
Apologies necessary to the scenery that may never be viewed,
Maybe the Wonderwall can save me and I'll have time now to alter my mood.

27/04/08

use the sword

Like a double edged sword actions cut in the worst way,
While personally defending the offence, decisions are ambiguous,
No matter how the situation is viewed, losing is inevitable,
But skill defies the storyline earning recognition,
Victory accompanies whomever brings never ending ammunition,

What was meant as simple compliments gets blown out of proportion,
The mind's anxiety fills with bitter toxin,
Like nail on slate the screech is deafening,
Escape from maladaptive thoughts leaves tender lungs in pain while screaming,
What was asked is something more than demeaning,

Using a sharp mind has some advantage,
Symbolic of the sword, a mind's precision is its strength,
Putting thought into word makes sense to the poet,
Speedy cognitions inspire divinity in speech,
Speech remains silent while the friendship seems breached,

27/04/08

grins overwhelming

Complexion transforms as the face flush previews the contraction,
Understanding the actions, now history, rest comfortably in the kiln,
When fire changes earth to ivory, love changes the bond,
Peeking behind the curtains reveals the road to salvation.

As the molecules bind complete satisfaction is witnessed,
Another body acts as the catalyst,
The reflection of the grin demands more of the same,
Being with her inspires marathon efforts while playing the game.

Living in the moment while a smile exists is something euphoric,
The grins anticipated surround what will surely be historic,
Just the thought of her name is beautifully melodic,
A panoramic landscape is more than just a dream that is scenic.

Reading electronic compositions brings with it splendid emotions,
As personal as blood the void needs to be filled with the number 9 potion,
Trust maintained invites the reaction entailing an overwhelming grin,
Two souls homogenize over time; thus, guaranteeing the win.

28/04/08

possibilities

The possibilities are hopes, dreams and aspirations all rolled into one,
Possibility thinking is facilitated by calmness and composure,
Withdrawing from the Rat Race encouraged by Media clarifies,
Daily clarity makes the journey worth living until the time here is done,

When life's batteries run low and expire the game is only in intermission,
Like changing batteries the soul is put into a new home to keep learning,
Each life is a step along the stairway to heaven where each heaven is individual,
These possibilities granted from the Almighty Power's digression,

Faith in the possibilities materializes a security really only dreamed of,
This security comes from within yet is understood as coming from above,
This security is also born of the emotion generated by love,
A lot like the life brought to Columbus in the beak of the dove,

We're all here to explore our possibilities while learning to achieve divinity,
Approaching the vibrations that escape fear entertains the possibility,
Accepting the possibility of fantastic life avoids negativity,
Living life enthusiastically, modestly, provides lofty cognitions of serendipity,

Being the recipient of these possibilities equates to a life of happiness with ease,
Paying attention to the message heard inspires communication while on knees,
The sun is shining on a life now privileged enough to be entrusted with the keys,
Certainly this knowledge and understanding is what our society needs,

29/04/08

inspirations

Enjoying thoughts that use the brain as their playground,
Life moves in cyclic cycles like those of the Merry-go-round,
Up and down, life's routines take while the wooden horses copy on their poles,
Certain inspirations come encrypted inviting suitors to realize their goals.

There's inspiration in tragedies once accepted,
Inspiring relationships are with patience then built,
Time spent in contemplation is too often neglected,
From beauty, inspirations come, while their purity lacks guilt.

Inspired by you, a future tailed by a shooting star, can be realized,
All experience, through carefully crafted script, will be summarized,
Living today demands inspiration for the next moment to occur,
That moment is found simply by entrusting all emotions to her.

Wondrous sparkle observed in her eyes anticipates adventure to live in clarity,
Ponderous cognitions keep both hemispheres exhausted with everything happy,
Magnificent dreams of noble promiscuity give slumber the quality to miss,
All storms are silenced with the inspiration accompanied by a solitary kiss.

1/05/08

that face

Sitting here while being watched keeps grins surfacing,
Keeping honest vigil, the face reminds me of a London Guard,
Stretching the mind while resting firmly comfortable on the ground,
Her voice echoes in the vibrations-following every sound.

Perched over my right shoulder, what could be an angel, waits,
The beginning is soon to take place on the other side of the gates,
Looking forward to the previews keeps me on the edge of an abyss,
My stomach suffering from anxiety's eternal bliss,

Leonardo painted that face encoding enchanted mystery,
The face now in majestic beauty captures glances from all who see,
As a true wonderwall Oasis never dreamed this beauty could be reality,
Living through penance is similar to the time before the fall of eternity.

10/04/08

volume three:
"haiku"

careful investigation

They are painful but
Relationships can fulfill
The fun of the game

26/03/07

choices

Choices run the world
Matter of fact envisioned
Make the right choice count

12/03/08

untitled

Cavan memories
That place never to forget
Situational Smells

23/04/08

fatigue

When everything hurts
And slumber won't transpire
Body begs to rest

10/03/08

untitled

Feeling left behind
Drained body, spirit, and mind,
The wish to rewind

20/04/08

finding reality

Only be yourself
Putting faith in what matters
Means understanding

07/04/08

got to believe

Believe in something
Why not believe in me?
Got to have a belief

27/03/08

idea's road map

To infer meaning
Placing opinion forward
Cognitions playground

27/03/08

indecision

The question at hand
Should we stay or should we go
Make up your mind please

12/03/08

jedi ways

Living without time
Ambassador for new life
At one with the force

12/04/08

lent

Lost for forty days
Practice brings closer to God
Found in forty days

13/03/08

love

Glands vomit for you
For lubrication we need
Insert and Enjoy

13/03/08

love's truth

You can't hurry love
Unbelievable feelings
You just have to wait

14/04/08

lust

Lotions invite use
For lubrication we need
Insert and Enjoy

13/03/08

nature

Distinctly Human
All reason attributed
Excuse for all things

27/03/08

nava armani

There's Beauty in sight
Catalyst for reaction
She draws great feelings

20-03-08

naveed

That beautiful smile
Unusually vivid
Flash Bulb Memory

03/22/08

nudity

Beautiful to see
Keeps minds always occupied
Sexual to touch

13/04/08

plan for survival

Being day or night
Positive thoughts infiltrate
With you forever

02/04/08

poetic ability

From where not knowing
The words are coming to me
To express secrets

26/03/08

soul mate

Bound relationship
The future is together
Every kiss to come

13/03/08

untitled

Survivor's story
Dealing with inequities
Then you rise above

14/04/08

the white stump

Live among giants
Nowhere to run so stay put
To just admire life

12/03/08

writing

While the world sleeps
Feverish cognitions laps
The mind works on Haiku

13/03/08

personal gift

From where not knowing
The words are coming to me
To express secrets

26/03/08

cranial strength

Thinking cognitions
Such acts promote confidence
The energy speaks

26/03/08

ISBN 142518134-1